MORGELLONS: LEVEL 5 PLAGUE OF THE NEW WORLD ORDER

DOCTORS SAY IT IS ALL IN THEIR HEADS - BUT THE VICTIMS KNOW IT IS HORRIFYINGLY REAL!

COMMANDER X & TIM R. SWARTZ

MORGELLONS: LEVEL 5 PLAGUE OF THE NEW WORLD ORDER

INNER LIGHT/GLOBAL COMMUNICATIONS

MORGELLONS: LEVEL 5 PLAGUE OF THE NEW WORLD ORDER

By
Commander X & Tim R. Swartz

Timothy Green Beckley: Editorial Director
Carol Rodriguez: Publishers Assistant
Cover Art: Tim Swartz

Global Communications
P.O. Box 753
New Brunswick, NJ 08903

Subscribe to our free e-mail newsletter at:
www.conspiracyjournal.com

CONTENTS

CHAPTER ONE
THE FIBER DISEASE
PAGE 3

•

CHAPTER TWO
THE BIOWARFARE CONSPIRACY
PAGE 13

•

CHAPTER THREE
WAS MOGELLONS DEVELOPED IN A LAB?
PAGE 29

•

CHAPTER FOUR
IS MORGELLONS FROM OUTER SPACE?
PAGE 37

•

CHAPTER FIVE
ALL IN THEIR HEADS
PAGE 46

CHAPTER ONE
The Fiber Disease

A mysterious skin disease is currently spreading across the United States, but many doctors are not sure if it is real or just in the heads of the sufferers. It is called Morgellons and the symptoms sound as if they could have been lifted straight from the pages of a science fiction book.

Those with this disease describe feelings insects scuttling beneath their skin and have mysterious sores that ooze out blue and white fibers, some as thick as spaghetti strands. Attempts to remove the fibers are said to elicit shooting pains radiating from the site.

The lesions range from minor to disfiguring in appearance and the fibers appear either as single strands or as bundles. Patients also sometimes report the presence of fibers or black granular specks on their skin even in the absence of lesions.

According to a news report from KTVU-TV in Oakland, CA, Former Oakland A's pitcher Billy Koch has the disease, as does his wife and three children. Koch had to leave baseball at age 29 partly because of the uncontrollable muscle twitching that went on for months at a time and kept up him up all night.

The couple was at their wit's end after numerous doctors not only provided little in the way of relief, but actually were skeptical about their health problems. The Kochs may be the most recognizable of more than 3,000 families nationwide reporting these same unexplained symptoms. However, there are curious clusters of those suffering from the disease, in Florida along the Gulf Coast of Texas, and in California's San Francisco Bay Area.

To date, no clinical studies have looked into Morgellons and the first paper mentioning Morgellons was published in a recent issue of the **American Journal of Clinical Dermatology**, co-authored by members of the Morgellons Research Foundation, a non-profit organization devoted to raising public awareness about the disease. The disease is named after a medical condition described in 1674 by the British author Thomas Browne. Known as "Morgellons," Browne said the disorder caused children to "critically break out with harsh hairs on their backs." However, the Morgellons Research Foundation says that it is doubtful that the 17th-century disease is related to modern-day Morgellons.

Analysis of the fibers found in the sores suggest that they are more than just lint from clothing, carpets, or bedding, nor are the black specks composed of pepper, as several dermatologists have proposed. Some suggest the fibers are made of cellulose, a molecule generally found in plants. And if placed in a petri dish, the fibers taken from a Margellons sore will continue to grow.

Surprisingly, most of the medical community seems to think that Morgellons is mass delusion and most people complaining of the symptoms are diagnosed with "delusional parasitosis," a psychological problem in which people imagine that they are infested with parasites. Yet patients a continent apart have reported the same symptoms long before hearing about the disease in the media or talking to other patients with similar symptoms.

THE MYSTERY DISEASE

According to a June, 2006 report on KHOU-TV in Houston, Texas, 59-year-old Cheryall Spiller suffers from what she believes is a mystery disease.

"Small white worms that come out of my ears, you can feel them itching in there. You can get a Q-tip and dig them out," she explained.

Spiller is not alone with her complaints. Other people also say that they have something strange under their skin.

"The sores come up and these fuzzy, thread-like things come out," said Stephanie Bailey, Austin resident. "It's almost like spores or something like that."

Lesions and scars cover Stephanie Bailey's arms and legs. Travis Wilson is a victim as well.

"It feels just like bugs are crawling all over you. You can't sleep. It's freaky. So he'd go days without sleep," said Lisa Wilson, the patient's mother.

According to nurse practitioner Ginger Savely, all three may have an emerging sickness called Morgellons disease.

"It just looks you know like somebody picked at something and it got a little infected," Savely said.

Morgelleons: Level 5 Plague of the New World Order

Sufferers of Mogellons have taken their complaints to doctors. When magnified 60 times, the sores take on a completely different look.

"So you focus a little more you can see the black fibers the white fibers," Savely said.

Savely admitted the idea of creatures living inside our bodies seems more like science fiction than science.

"I don't think a person can believe it until they see it with their own eyes," she said. "The problem is people aren't looking hard enough, most practitioners are not looking because they are not taking them seriously."

Mainstream medical professionals don't believe Morgellons is real.

"I think if we look at what is truly evidence-based medicine, what has been proven based on scientific fact we know we don't have a means to substantiate her observations," said Dr. Adelaide Hebert, U.T. Health Science Center Houston.

Dr. Adelaide Hebert said Morgellons exists only in the patient's mind.

"Many of these patients do have delusion of parasitosis," Dr. Hebert said. "It is actually not uncommon to have patients come in and describe the sensation that something is crawling on their skin."

KHOU-TV searched for a Houston doctor who believes in or treats Morgellons, but none could be found. At Oklahoma State University research is currently underway on a volunteer basis. Ginger Savely has documented 100 cases and treats her patients with oral and topical antibiotics.

"They can't get anybody to help them in the medical profession. It's just a nightmare, a living nightmare. I can't imagine any worse disease," she said.

Lisa Wilson's son became so distraught about his condition he took his own life two weeks ago.

"He would tell me he'd rather have cancer because then he'd know what he was up against," Lisa Wilson said.

"They're worried about the bird flu coming, you've got something here right now that's spreadable and it's being hush-hushed," Spiller said.

"They told me I was doing it to myself and that I was nuts," Bailey explained. "I stopped going to doctors because I was afraid they were going to lock me up."

For most doctors, Morgellons is a textbook example of a type of mental illness where the victim believes that they are covered in parasites. This belief among doctors is so prevalent that few even bother to take the time to interview the sufferers of Morgellons, much less examine their skin lesions or look at the strange threads and fibers that ooze from their ulcers. However, Morgellons, or the Fiber Disease as some are calling it, is quickly spreading across the planet and the media is finally taking notice.

FORMER OAKLAND A'S PITCHER HAS MORGELLONS

Former Oakland A's pitcher Billy Koch has Morgellons. And so do his wife and their three children. And though they can afford top medical care, doctors have no answers according to a news report by KTVU.

It started in Oakland four years ago. Koch saved 44 games and was the top reliever in the major leagues. His fastball wowed crowds. And then the strangeness began.

"He freaked out. He wanted to ignore it I wanted to too. But when it comes to your kids, you gotta stop ignoring it," said Koch's wife Brandi.

She describes their symptoms: "It was the scariest thing I had ever realized in my entire life. There were threads and black specks coming out and off of my skin."

Within two years, at age 29, Billy Koch was out of baseball, partly because of the uncontrollable muscle twitching that went on for months at a time and often kept up him up all night. The disease is characterized by slow healing skin lesions that often extrude small, dark filaments, especially after bathing.

"That's when it would really just ooze, literally ooze out of my skin," explained Brandi Koch.

The couple was at wit's end after numerous doctors not only provided little in the way of relief, but actually were skeptical about their health problems: "There's no reasonable explanation for it. I'm not seeing things. I'm watching it happen. We're pretty sane people" lamented Billy.

Infectious disease specialist Dr. Neelam Uppal sympathized with the Kochs' plight: "They've seen several doctors, and everybody's told them they're crazy. It's all in their head. They're delusional. That is the doctors that took the time to see them; most would not even bother too see their patients."

Dr. Uppal gave the Kochs and fifteen other patients a powerful anti-parasite medicine and antibiotics that helped temporarily. But the filaments come back.

Testing of the filaments brought no results, according to Dr. Uppal: "I've seen it; sent it to the lab. They can't identify it. They'll say 'They're nothing.'"

Morgelleons: Level 5 Plague of the New World Order

The reaction of medical professionals has made a difficult situation even harder for Brandi Koch: "It's not enough that you're suffering and hurting. It's 'You're an idiot!' and 'You're crazy!' on top of it. I'm really hurt and sad and scared."

The Kochs may be the most recognizable of more than 3,000 families nationwide reporting these same unexplained symptoms. There are curious clusters, in Florida, along the Gulf Coast and in the San Francisco Bay Area.

San Francisco physician Rafael Stricker took samples in the spring of 2006 from Bay Area sufferers. Patients report pustules and filaments that most doctors dismiss. Dermatologists claimed the filaments were all delusions, although none had studied them.

Oklahoma State University Professor Randy Wymore was the first scientist to conduct research on this disconcerting disease. He says it is the biggest mystery he's ever been involved in.

The UC Davis trained physiologist is leading a medical team at Oklahoma State University in Tulsa, researching the bizarre disease. With cooperation from the Centers for Disease Control and Prevention, Wymore's team is studying Bay Area patients and others from around the country. His first finding disputes the frequent diagnosis of delusions of parasites.

"Pathologists and dermatologists and lab reports said that these were textile fibers appearing in the skin of the sufferers: pieces of lint, threads from clothes or carpeting. Now that's just not true, to be perfectly blunt about it," says Prof. Wymore.

Wymore says his tests rule out not only textile fibers, but also worms, insects, animal material and even human skin and hair. He says the filaments are not an external contamination.

Instead, they are a substance that materializes somehow inside the body, apparent artifacts of something infectious. More results are expected soon. And Wymore says skin problems are not the worst symptoms.

He says a neurotoxin or microorganism may disturb muscle control and memory.

"The neurological effects are the much more severe, life altering and much more dangerous of the conditions," explains Prof. Wymore.

In June of 2006, Georgia began a statewide Morgellons registry. Prof. Wymore says he is about to begin a clinical trial and offers this to sufferers: "We know there's something going on here. You're not delusional."

Prof. Wymore has released an open letter to doctors treating patients with Morgellons symptoms. It asks physicians to take it seriously, saying these patients are likely suffering from a still untreatable emerging disease.

Morgelleons: Level 5 Plague of the New World Order

May 15, 2006
Re: Morgellons Disease

From: Randy S. Wymore, Ph.D., Department of Pharmacology & Physiology, Rhonda Casey, D.O., Department of Pediatrics Oklahoma State University Center for Health Sciences, Tulsa, Oklahoma

Dear Practitioner,

This letter concerns a patient population that manifests a particular set of symptoms we have encountered with increasing frequency, and that OSU-CHS is actively researching. The condition has been labeled as Morgellons Disease and it is unclear if this is a single disease or a multi-faceted syndrome.

Until recently, most of these patients have been grouped as a subset of the diagnosis of Delusions of Parasites (delusional parasitosis; DOP). After obtaining careful patient histories and thorough physical exam, we have determined that Morgellons patients have several important distinctions ruling out the diagnosis of DOP.

This population of patients frequently exhibits the following symptoms:

• Distinct and poorly healing skin lesions with unusually thick, membranous scarring upon eventual healing.

• Moderate to extreme pruritis at sites of lesions as well as un-erupted skin.

• Microscopic examination of these lesions will most often reveal the presence of unusual fibers, which may be black, blue or red. These fibers, which many healthcare providers initially thought to be textile contaminants, are often present in the deep tissue of biopsies obtained from unbroken skin of individuals with this condition. Careful examination of these fibers further reveals that they are frequently associated with hair follicles, and are definitely not textile in origin.

• Most of these patients suffer from a host of neurological symptoms which can vary in severity from mild to severe. These neurological symptoms include peripheral tingling, paresthesias and varying degrees of motor involvement which appear to progress.

8

Morgelleons: Level 5 Plague of the New World Order

• Intermittent cognitive and behavioral status changes are often observed and also seem to progress with the severity of disease. This is often referred to as "brain fog" by the patient as they experience a waxing and waning of this symptom.

• Laboratory findings in these patients are variable, but often reveal eosinophilia and elevated levels of Immunoglobin E.

• Other symptoms of varying severity and frequency have been described, and are included in the attached case definition.

Morgellons patients differ from classical, delusional parasitosis patients in several areas. They do not respond to antipsychotics, and new lesions continue to appear upon complete cessation of manual excoriation.

Due to the sensation of foreign material in their tissue, that has been described as sharp, stinging and/or splinter-like, the patient may have discovered the fibers prior to seeking medical care, and may bring them to your office for examination. Please do not assume that the patient's problem is purely psychological based on this propensity.

Many of these patients may appear skeptical of traditional medical care due to frequent dismissal of their symptoms in the past. The combination of suffering from a chronic disease with distressful symptoms and no known cause or cure can cause some patients to appear anxious or agitated.

We encourage you to take the time to carefully interview any patient who may fall into this category, perform any testing you may deem appropriate, and most importantly treat the patient with compassion and dignity.

Sincerely,

Randy S. Wymore, Ph.D.

Rhonda Casey, D.O.

Director of Research,

Associate Professor of Pediatrics

Morgellons Research Foundation

Assistant Professor of Pharmacology

Oklahoma State University - Center for Health Sciences

1111 West 17th Steet, Tulsa, Oklahoma 74107-1898

E-mail: morgellons@okstate.edu

Morgellons Information Line: (877) 599-7999

www.healthsciences.okstate.edu/morgellons/index.cfm

Morgelleons: Level 5 Plague of the New World Order

A TYPICAL CASE

Another typical case is Betty Armour, who is afraid to wear shorts and afraid of what people might think if they saw her condition. She is afraid of what they might say to her if she told them her truth.

"I have Morgellons disease," she would say.

From the knees down, Armour isn't herself, and she hasn't been for two and a half years. The fronts of her legs are noticeably discolored and bruised. It's a mixture of brown and purplish-looking scar tissue with pimply sores that itch and sting sometimes, says the 42-year-old Armour.

The wounds are so close together, they look like trails leading nowhere. "I think they have a wiry, suture quality to them," she said.

The Rancho Cucamonga, California woman has had similar, bizarre skin "lesions," for lack of a more descriptive or all-encompassing word, on her ankles, arms, breasts and hands. Painful sores on the tips of her fingers swelled up over Armour's nails and obstructed regular growth. Picking at them helped relieve tension, she says; today, they look fairly healthy.

She had similar swelling on her feet; her shoe size has gone from size 8 to 10.

At first, Armour thought she had come down with her second bout of lichen planus, a relatively common skin disease that afflicted her 15 years ago and is possibly linked to stress, experts say. Lichen planus usually fades, however, and although Armour's lesions have changed over time, they certainly aren't all gone.

Fruitless research ensued until a May 20, 2006 television broadcast on a local station opened Armour's eyes to Morgellons. Further, she found there to be more than 4,500 registered households listed on the Morgellons Research Foundation Web site.

The segment touched upon most of the symptoms Armour says she suffers, such as fatigue, joint pain and difficulty concentrating. This trio is so debilitating sometimes, a career beyond taking care of her teenagers – ages 15, 17, 19 – and miniature poodle seems like a pipe dream.

Before her health problems began, Armour, who grew up in La Puente, was an administrator at an area Longs Drugs distribution center for nearly a decade.

"I look forward to getting back to work, but I wouldn't hire me right now," Armour said.

According to research published in the American Journal of Clinical Dermatology, Morgellons disease is characterized by poorly healing skin lesions with thick, membranous scarring as well as fiberlike strands extruding from the lesions. Armour describes her fibers, which come off pretty easily, as cottonlike, fuzzy and many shades: beige, black, green and white. She's retained fiber samples in Ziploc bags and plastic containers, including "suturelike" fibers she's coughed up.

"It's getting very frustrating when people tell me I don't know what I'm talking about," she said. "I know it's real, I have the evidence."

Armour's children live with her, hug her and, fortunately, have not exhibited any of the six characteristic symptoms of Morgellons, as defined in the research foundation's case definition presented to the Centers for Disease Control and Prevention on Feb. 14, 2006:

1. Intensely itchy skin lesions, both appearing spontaneously and self-generated.

2. Crawling sensations conceptualized by the patient as bugs moving, stinging or biting, intermittently.

3. Fatigue.
4. Cognitive difficulties.

5. Behavioral effects, as many Morgellons patients have been diagnosed with attention-deficit (hyperactivity) disorder, bipolar disorder, obsessive-compulsive disorder or something similar.

6. Fibers.

Limited research has tried to link the skin ailment to Lyme disease as well as antibacterial therapy. Since Armour began seeking treatment two and a half years ago, physicians at her usual medical facility - PrimeCare of Inland Valley in Rancho Cucamonga - have neither alleviated her symptoms nor diagnosed her with anything more than dermatitis.

"I brought up Morgellons with one doctor," she said, "but he thought I was bonkers and wouldn't hear of it."

Without public outreach, Armour can't do much but wait. She longs to, but hasn't met or talked with anyone who suffers her symptoms. She wants to meet other with Morgellons and figure out what may have caused the disease, what the common denominators are.

Morgelleons: Level 5 Plague of the New World Order

Practically all sufferers of Morgellons are reluctant to talk about their illness because they know that some people would think they are crazy. And that is exactly what most doctors do think: As far as they know, Morgellons is not a recognized disease, at this point, at least.

"I've seen colors of some of these fibers. Some of them are bright blue," said Dr. Vincent De Leo, program director of the dermatology department at St. Luke's-Roosevelt Hospital Center in New York.

"There is nothing in the body that is bright blue. So it has to be something from the environment. And some of them are fibers, but they're fibers I believe from the environment, not from inside the skin."

De Leo and many others believe the lesions are self-inflicted, caused by scratching because the patients have a psychiatric disorder where they wrongly believe their bodies are infested with parasites.

"And then they begin to focus on those lesions and try to get them better, usually by picking out the fibers or the bugs or whatever it is," De Leo said.

Morgellons exhibits such bizarre symptoms that it is no wonder that physicians fail to recognize it as a real disease. Perhaps that is the plan by those who want the disease to spread unnoticed and unchecked until it is finally too late.

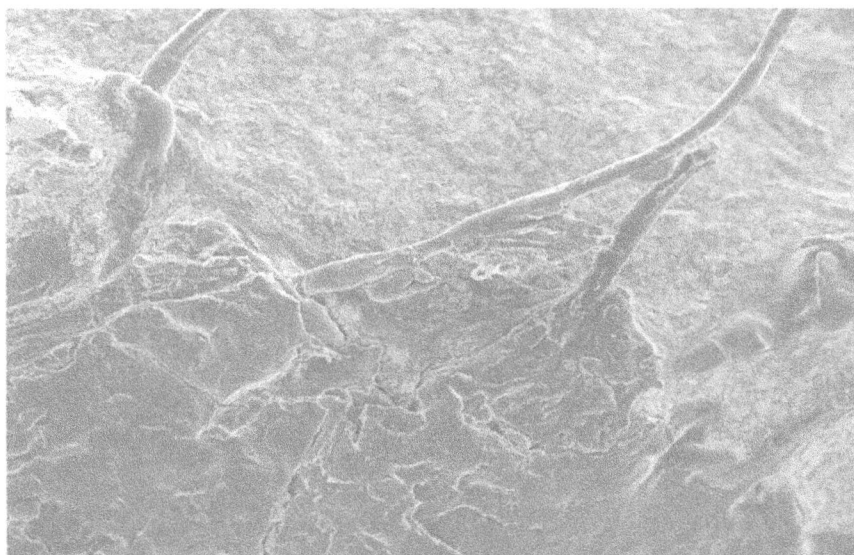

Bizarre thread-like fibers are one of the symptoms of Morgellons. Seen here under an electron microscope emerging from the skin.

CHAPTER TWO
The Biowarfare Conspiracy

There is a long and sordid history of the manmade manipulation of natural diseases for the use in war. It is natural to suspect any strange illness that seems to surface out of nowhere as the product of a mad experiment gone wrong and released on an unsuspecting population.

Take for example the latest manmade disease created by Mark Buller of the University of St Louis. His team deliberately produced an extremely lethal form of mousepox, a relative of the smallpox virus, one of the most deadly viruses on earth.

Financed by the National Institute of Allergy and Infectious Diseases, the research project was supposed to help find new protection against smallpox, which kills one in three victims. Unfortunately, it seems that there may have been other motives for the development of this virus.

Buller's new genetically altered mousepox virus kills all mice, even if they have been given antiviral drugs and a vaccine which would normally protect them. In addition, the cowpox virus, which also infects humans, has also been genetically manipulated under the pretense "that this work is necessary to explore what bioterrorists might do," says Buller.

According to *New Scientist*, Ian Ramshaw of the Australian National University said, "I have great concern about doing this in a pox virus that can cross species."

It has long been suspected that the HIV virus that causes AIDS was created for the use in biowarfare. This has long been the poster child for conspiracy theorists worldwide; however, respected doctors and scientists also suspect that there is more to HIV than a simple cross-species transference.

The first African woman to win the Nobel Peace Prize, Wangari Maatha of Kenya, has spoken out on the AIDS virus saying it was man-made and deliberateloy created as a weapon of biowarfare.

"In fact it (the HIV virus) is created by a scientist for biological warfare," she said. "Why has there been so much secrecy about AIDS? When you ask: where did the virus come from? it raises a lot of flags. That makes me suspicious," Maathai said.

The Kenya based *East Africa Standard* reported that in response to questions from Asian and European media, she said, "I want to dedicate the prize the African woman. I want to hold and embrace her. She has suffered so much and I feel this is an honor to her."

"Although I am a biologist, I have not done any research. I may not be able to say who developed the (HIV) virus but it was meant to wipe out the Black race," she continued.

When she first blamed the HIV/Aids on "some sadistic scientists, Professor Maathai kicked a storm, leaving some experts outraged and others supporting her," the Standard reported.

AIDS AS A WEAPON

William Campbell Douglass, MD, in his article *WHO Murdered Africa (The Man Made Origin of AIDS)* says that the World Health Organisation in published articles, called for scientists to work with deadly agents such as retro viruses and attempt to make a hybrid virus that would be deadly to humans.

In the bulletin of the World Health Organisation WHO), Volume 47, p.259, 1972, they said, "An attempt should be made to see if viruses can in fact exert selective effects on immune function. The possibility should be looked into that the immune response to the victims itself may be impaired if the infecting virus damages, more or less selectively, the cell responding to the virus."

What the WHO is saying in plain English is "Let's cook up a virus that selectively destroys the T-cell system of man, an acquired immune deficiency." In other words, AIDS.

Dr. Boyd E. Graves postulates that AIDS was the culmination of biowarfare research conducted by the U.S. Government (and later, by the Soviet government) throughout the 20th century. He believes AIDS was developed and proliferated for the primary purpose of wiping out blacks, homosexuals, and other social groups considered being "excess population."

Dr. Graves has also suggested that Gulf War syndrome may be related to AIDS which was spread by contaminating soldiers with vaccines, and that an effective cure for AIDS has already been developed and patented but is being withheld. The evidence Graves cites that AIDS was developed in U.S. was based on a 1971 Special Virus Cancer Flow Chart that he obtained through the Freedom of Information Act.

Graves claims to have contracted AIDS, but was cured by a single injection of Tetrasilver Tetroxide (Ag404) - not colloidal silver (see U.S. Patent #5,676,977 "Method of curing AIDS with tetrasilver tetroxide molecular crystal devices" held by Marantech. Graves, however, admits his diagnosis may have been a false positive. However, the claims made in the patent have not been investigated by any mainstream scientific body.

Dr. Alan Cantwell, author of ***AIDS and the Doctors of Death: An Inquiry into the Origin of the AIDS Epidemic***, and, ***Queer Blood: The Secret AIDS Genocide Plot***, believes that HIV is a genetically modified organism developed by U.S. Government scientists; that it was introduced into the population through Hepatitis B experiments performed on gay and bisexual men between 1978-1981 in Manhattan, Los Angeles, San Francisco, St. Louis, Denver, and Chicago. Cantwell claims these experiments were directed by Dr. Wolf Szmuness; and that there is an ongoing government and media cover-up regarding the origin of the AIDS epidemic.

Matilde Krim, a cancer virologist, AIDS expert, and the co-chairperson of the American Foundation for AIDS Research, has also suggested that Dr. Wolf Szmuness' hepatitis B vaccination experiments of the late 70's caused the AIDS epidemic. Unlike Cantwell, however, she attributes this to accident rather than conspiracy.

Dr. Gary Glum claims in his book ***Full Disclosure*** that he received top secret information that AIDS was made in the laboratory at Cold Spring Harbor, New York. The virus was spread by putting the AIDS viruses into the smallpox eradication program by the World Health Organization, and that AIDS did not exist before 1978.

AIDS, he claims, was created for population control, especially of Blacks, Asians, and other colored people. The people who control the project were people known as the Olympians (another name for the Illuminati), who are also supporting eugenics. Organizations such as Red Cross are, according to Glum, complicit in the conspiracy by not testing blood properly. Glum also believes that AIDS can be transmitted through kissing, mosquito bites and casual contact.

Glum reports that Upjohn Pharmaceuticals tested a number of substances that can treat AIDS, but that the results have been suppressed.

Much of Glum's evidence is based upon anecdotal claims, and critics have reported a complete absence of medical evidence to support his claims.

Dr. Leonard G. Horowitz, author of ***Emerging Viruses: AIDS & Ebola, Nature, Accident or Intentional?*** and ***Death in the Air: Globalism, Terrorism and Toxic Warfare***, has advanced the theory that the AIDS virus was engineered by such U.S. Government defense contractors as Litton Bionetics for the purposes of bio-warfare and "population control."

Dr. Horowitz believes that Jews, blacks, and Hispanics are prime targets in these attempts at "population control." He cites the historical preoccupation with eugenics on the part of the American medical establishment as evidence of a greater conspiracy to commit genocide.

It should be pointed out that the former Soviet Union, in a plot to destabilize the Western world, planted disinformation suggesting the CIA or other agencies created AIDS. According to KGB defector Vasili Mitrokhin, the KGB originated the claim through an East German physicist, Jakob Segal, in the mid 1980s. Because of this, any evidence that a new disease is a manmade conspiracy should always be treated with caution.

THE SICKENING HISTORY OF BIOWARFARE

Biological warfare, also known as germ warfare, is the use of any organism (bacteria, virus or other disease-causing organism) or toxin found in nature, as a weapon of war. It is meant to incapacitate or kill an adversary.

The creation and stockpiling of biological weapons is outlawed by the 1972 Biological Weapons Convention, signed by over 100 states, because a successful attack could conceivably result in thousands, possibly even millions, of deaths and could cause severe disruptions to societies and economies. Oddly enough, the convention prohibits only creation and storage, but not usage, of these weapons. However, the consensus among military analysts is that, except in the context of bioterrorism, biological warfare is militarily of little use.

The main problem is that a biological warfare attack would take days to implement, and therefore, unlike a nuclear or chemical attack, would not immediately stop an advancing army. As a strategic weapon, biological warfare is again militarily problematic, because unless it is used to poison enemy civilian towns, it is difficult to prevent the attack from spreading, either to allies or to the attacker, and a biological warfare attack invites immediate massive retaliation, usually in the same form.

Morgelleons: Level 5 Plague of the New World Order

The use of biological agents is not new, but before the 20th century, biological warfare took three main forms:

- Deliberate poisoning of food and water with infectious material.
- Use of microorganisms, toxins or animals, living or dead, in a weapon system.
- Use of biologically inoculated fabrics.

Biological warfare has been practiced repeatedly throughout history. During the 6th Century B.C., The Assyrians poisoned enemy wells with a fungus that would make the enemy delusional and unable to fight in battle. In 184 BC, Hannibal of Carthage had clay pots filled with poisonous snakes and instructed his soldiers to throw the pots onto the decks of Pergamene ships.

Historical accounts from medieval Europe detail the use of infected animal carcasses, by Mongols, Turks and other groups, to infect enemy water supplies. Prior to the bubonic plague epidemic known as the Black Death, Mongol and Turkish armies were reported to have catapulted diseased corpses into besieged cities.

During the Middle Ages, victims of the bubonic plague were used for biological attacks, often by flinging their corpses and excrement over castle walls using catapults. The last known incident of using plague corpses for biological warfare occurred in 1710, when Russian forces attacked the Swedes by using catapults to fling plague-infected corpses over the city walls of Reval.

Much, or even most of the Native American population was decimated after contact with the Old World due to the introduction of many different fatal diseases. The British army at least once used smallpox as weapon, when they gave contaminated blankets to the Lenape. It is suspected but not confirmed that biological warfare was used against the Indians at other times as well.

Native peoples in Aptos gave to Spaniards gifts of freshly cut flowers wrapped in leaves of poison oak.

During the United States Civil War, General Sherman reported that Confederate forces shot farm animals in ponds upon which the Union depended for drinking water.

Use of such weapons was banned in international law by the Geneva Protocol of 1925. The 1972 Biological and Toxin Weapons Convention extended the ban to almost all production, storage and transport. It is, however, believed that since the signing of the convention the number of countries capable of producing such weapons has increased.

During the Sino-Japanese War (1937-1945) and World War II, Unit 731 of the Imperial Japanese Army conducted human experimentation on thousands, mostly Chinese. In military campaigns, the Japanese army used biological weapons on Chinese soldiers and civilians.

This employment was largely viewed as ineffective due to inefficient delivery systems. However, new information has surfaced within the last decade, which alleges a more active Japanese usage. For example, firsthand accounts testify the Japanese infected civilians through the distribution of plagued foodstuffs, such as dumplings, rice, bread and vegetables.

There are also reports of contaminated water supplies. Such estimates report over 580,000 victims, largely due to plague and cholera outbreaks. In addition, repeated seasonal outbreaks after the conclusion of the war bring the death toll much higher.

In response to suspected biological weapons development in Germany and Japan, the United States, United Kingdom, and Canada initiated a BW development program in 1941 that resulted in the weaponization of anthrax, brucellosis, and botulinum toxin. The center for U.S. military BW research was Fort Detrick, Maryland. Some biological and chemical weapons defense research was also conducted at Dugway Proving Grounds in Utah. Research carried out in the United Kingdom during World War II left a Scottish Island contaminated with anthrax for the next 48 years.

When biological and chemical weapons become too old, they sometimes need to be disposed of. Many NATO nations use the U.S. chemical weapons disposal facility on the tiny Johnston Atoll located in the middle of the Pacific.

Considerable research on the topic was performed by the United States, the Soviet Union, and probably other major nations throughout the Cold War era, though it is generally believed that such weapons were never used. This view was challenged by China and North Korea, who accused the United States of large-scale field testing of biological weapons against them during the Korean War (1950-1953).

Their accusation is substantiated by Stephen Endicott and Edward Hagerman in *The United States and Biological Warfare: secrets of the early Cold War and Korea* (Bloomington, Indiana University Press, 1998). In 1972, the U.S. signed the Biological and Toxic Weapons Convention, which banned "development, production, stockpiling, and use of microbes or their poisonous products except in amounts necessary for protective and peaceful research."

In 1986, the U.S. government spent $42 million on research for developing defenses against infectious diseases and toxins, ten times more money than was spent in 1981. The money went to 24 U.S. universities in hopes of developing strains on anthrax, Rift Valley fever, Japanese encephalitis, tularemia, shigella, botulin, and Q fever. When the Biology Department at MIT voted to refuse Pentagon funds for biotech research, the Reagan administration forced it to reverse its decision by threatening to cut off other funds.

There have been reports that the United States Army has been developing weapons-grade anthrax spores at Dugway Proving Ground, a chemical and biological defense testing facility in Utah, since at least as early as 1992. Under the BWC, nations are permitted to develop small amounts of BW agents for the purpose of defensive research. The United States maintains a stated national policy of never using biological weapons under any circumstances since November 1969 President Nixon.

BIOLOGICAL WEAPONS CHARACTERISTICS

Ideal characteristics of biological weapons are high infectivity, high potency, availability of vaccines, and delivery as an aerosol. Diseases most likely to be considered for use as biological weapons are contenders because of their lethality (if delivered efficiently), and robustness (making aerosol delivery feasible). The biological agents used in biological weapons can often be manufactured quickly and easily. The primary difficulty is not the production of the biological agent but delivery in an infective form to a vulnerable target.

For example, anthrax is considered an excellent agent. We use it here for discussion because it is historically important, and enough information is public that this discussion can't be used as a manual. First, it forms hardy spores, perfect for dispersal aerosols.

Second, pneumonic (lung) infections of anthrax usually do not cause secondary infections in other people. Thus, the effect of the agent is usually confined to the target. A pneumonic anthrax infection starts with ordinary "cold" symptoms and quickly becomes lethal, with a fatality rate that is 80% or higher. Finally, friendly personnel can be protected with suitable antibiotics or vaccines.

A mass attack using anthrax would require the creation of aerosol particles of 1.5 to 5 micrometres. Too large and the aerosol would be filtered out by the respiratory system. Too small and the aerosol would be inhaled and exhaled. Also, at this size, nonconductive powders tend to clump and cling because of electrostatic charges. This hinders dispersion. So, the material must be treated with silica to insulate and discharge the charges. The aerosol must be delivered so that rain and sun does not rot it, and yet the human lung can be infected. There are other technological difficulties as well.

Diseases considered for weaponization, or known to be weaponized include anthrax, Ebola, Bubonic Plague, Cholera, Tularemia, Brucellosis, Q fever, Machupo, VEE, and Smallpox. Naturally-occurring toxins that can be used as weapons include Ricin, SEB, Botulism Toxin, and many Mycotoxins.

It is important to note that all of the classical and modern biological weapons organisms are animal diseases, the only exception being smallpox. Thus, in any use of biological weapons, it is highly likely that animals will become ill either simultaneously with, or perhaps earlier than humans.

In the largest biological weapons "accident" known, the anthrax outbreak in Sverdlovsk (now Yekaterinburg) in the Soviet Union in 1971, sheep became ill with anthrax as far as 200 kilometers from the release point of the organism from a military facility in the southeastern portion of the city (known as Compound 15 and still off limits to visitors today). As we all now know, anthrax is very effective as a biological terror weapon.

MORGELLONS AND LYME DISEASE

Often those unfortunate enough to suffer with the debilitating symptoms of Morgellons are also found to have contracted Lyme disease sometime in the past. Doctors are still trying to determine if there is a biological connection with the two, or if Morgellons is simply taking opportunity of an already compromised immune system.

It is interesting that there is a connection between Lyme disease and Morgellons. This considering the attention Lymes has garnered with certain health professionals who feel that Lymes is not an ordinary illness.

Dr. Donald MacArthur, who was in charge of the development and testing of biological weapons for the Pentagon, spoke at a hearing before a Subcommittee of the Committee on Appropriations in 1969. MacArthur puts it like this.

"Incapacitating agents are a more recent development and are largely in the research and development phase (in 1969). In fact, the prime emphasis in agent research and development is on developing better incapacitating agents. We are synthesizing new compounds and testing them in animals. I should mention that there is a rule of thumb we use. Before an agent can be classified as an incapacitant, we feel that the mortality should be very low. Therefore, the ratio of the lethal dose to the incapacitating dose has to be very high. Now this is a very technical job. We have some of the top scientists in the country working for years on how to get more effective incapacitating agents. It is not easy. An incapacitating agent imposes a greater logistic burden on the enemy when he has to look after the disabled people."

Dr. Joseph Burrascano, who has done extensive research on Lyme disease, presented testimony in 1993 to the Senate Hearing Committee on Lyme disease. Dr. Burrascano stated in his testimony that he feared repercussions for speaking out at the Hearing. Obviously his fears were justified as he was later investigated by the Office of Professional Medical Conduct in New York. Dr. Burrascano was finally vindicated and did not lose his license, but it raises questions on why doctor's who treat and speak out about Lymes, are finding themselves in the crosshairs of government persecution.

The Lyme Disease Conspiracy
by Joseph J. Burrascano, Jr., M.D.
Reprinted from Senate Committee Hearing on
Lyme Disease
August 5, 1993

There is a core group of university-based Lyme disease researchers and physicians whose opinions carry a great deal of weight. Unfortunately many of them act unscientifically and unethically. They adhere to outdated, self-serving views and attempt to personally discredit those whose opinions differ from their own. They exert strong ethically questionable influence on medical journals, which enables them to publish and promote articles that are badly flawed. They work with government agencies to bias the agenda of consensus meetings, and have worked to exclude from these meetings and scientific seminars those with alternate opinions. They behave this way for reasons of personal or professional gain, and are involved in obvious conflicts of interest.

This group promotes the idea that Lyme is a simple, rare illness that is easy to avoid, difficult to acquire, simple to diagnose, and easily treated and cured with 30 days or less of antibiotics.

The truth is that Lyme is the fastest growing infectious illness in this country after AIDS, with a cost to society measured in the billions of dollars. It can be acquired by anyone who goes outdoors, very often goes undiagnosed for months, years, or forever in some patients, and can render a patient chronically ill and even totally disabled despite what this core group refers to as "adequate" therapy. There have been deaths from Lyme disease.

They feel that when the patient fails to respond to their treatment regimens it is because the patient developed what they named "the post Lyme syndrome". They claim that this is not an infectious problem, but a rheumatologic or arthritic malady due to activation of the immune system.

The fact is this cannot be related to any consistent abnormality other than persistent infection. As further proof, vaccinated animals whose immune system has been activated by Lyme have never developed this syndrome. On the other hand, there is proof that persistent infection can exist in these patients because the one month treatment did not eradicate the infection.

Indeed, many chronically ill patients, whom these physicians dismissed, have gone on to respond positively and even recover, when additional antibiotics are given.

It is interesting that these individuals who promote this so called "post-Lyme syndrome" as a form of arthritis, depend on funding from arthritis groups and agencies to earn their livelihood. Some of them are known to have received large consulting fees from insurance companies to advise them to curtail coverage for any antibiotic therapy beyond this arbitrary 30 day cutoff, even if the patient will suffer. This is despite the fact that additional therapy may be beneficial, and despite the fact that such practices never occur in treating other diseases.

Morgelleons: Level 5 Plague of the New World Order

Following the lead of this group of physicians, a few state health departments have even begun to investigate, in a very threatening way, physicians who have more liberal views on Lyme disease diagnosis and treatment than they do. Indeed, I must confess that I feel that I am taking a large personal risk here today by publicly stating these views, for fear that I may suffer some negative repercussions, despite the fact that many hundreds of physicians and many thousands of patients all over the world agree with what I am saying here. Because of this bias by this inner circle, Lyme disease is both underdiagnosed and undertreated, to the great detriment to many of our citizens. Let me address these points in more detail.

UNDERDIAGNOSIS

1. Under reporting: The current reporting criteria for Lyme are inadequate and miss an estimated 30 to 50% of patients. Some states curtailed their active surveillance programs and saw an artificial drop in reported cases of nearly 40%, leading the uninformed to believe incorrectly that the number of new cases of Lyme is on the decline. The reporting procedure is often so cumbersome that many physicians never bother to report cases. Some physicians have found themselves unexpectedly the target of state health department investigators. Finally, to many physicians and government agents rely on the notoriously unreliable serologic blood test to confirm the diagnosis.

2. Poor Lyme disease diagnostic testing: It is very well-known that the serologic blood test for Lyme is insensitive, inaccurate, not standardized, and misses up to 40 percent of cases, yet many physicians, including many of those referred to above, and the senior staff at CDC and NIH, insist that if the blood test is negative, then the patient could not possibly have Lyme. This view is not supported by the facts. Lyme is diagnosed clinically, and can exist even when the blood test is negative.

The Rocky Mountain Lab of the NIH, which is the country's best government laboratory for Lyme research, had developed an excellent diagnostic test for this illness nearly 4 years ago, yet further work on it has been stalled due to lack of funding. Incredibly, if not for private donations of just $5,000 from the non-profit National Lyme Disease Foundation headquartered in Connecticut, then this research would have had to be abandoned. An additional $30,000 was donated by this organization to allow them to continue other valuable projects relating to vaccine development and disease pathogenesis. Yet, many physicians believe that thousands of dollars of grant moneys awarded by the government to other, outside researchers is poorly directed, supporting work of low relevance and low priority to those sick with Lyme. In spite of this, their funding continues, and the Rocky Mountain Lab is still underfunded.

3. The university and Government based Lyme establishment deny the existence of atypical presentations of Lyme and patients in this category are not being diagnosed or treated, and have no one to see and no place to go for proper care.

RESULTS: Some Lyme patients have had to see, as many as 42 different physicians often over several years, and at tremendous cost, before being properly diagnosed. Unfortunately, the disease was left to progress during that time, and patients were left forever ill, for by that time, their illness was not able to be cured. Even more disturbing, these hard line physicians have tried to dismiss these patients as having "Lyme Hysteria" and tried to claim they all were suffering from psychiatric problems!

UNDERTREATMENT

1. Because the diagnosis is not being made, for reasons partly outlined above.

2. University based and government endorsed treatment protocols are empiric, insufficient, refer to studies involving inadequate animal models, and are ignorant of basic pharmacology. They are not based on honest systematic studies or on the results of newer information.

3. After short courses of treatments with antibiotics, patients with advanced disease rarely return to normal, yet many can be proven to still be severely infected and can often respond to further, proper, antibiotic therapy. Unfortunately, many Lyme

patients are being routinely denied such therapy for political reasons and/or because insurance companies refuse to pay for longer treatment, upon the arbitrary and uninformed advice of these physicians, who are on the insurance company's payroll.

4. Long term studies on patients who were untreated or undertreated demonstrated the occurrence of severe illness more than a decade later, reminiscent of the findings of the notorious Tuskeege Study, in which intentionally untreated syphilis patients were allowed to suffer permanent and in some cases fatal sequelae.

5. The Lyme bacterium spreads to areas of the body that render this organism resistant to being killed by the immune system and by antibiotics, such as in the eye, deep within tendons, and within cells. The Lyme bacterium also has a very complex life cycle that renders it resistant to simple treatment strategies. Therefore, to be effective, antibiotics must be given in generous doses over several months, until signs of active infection have cleared. Because relapses have appeared long after seemingly adequate therapy, long term followup, measured in years or decades, is required before any treatment regimen is deemed adequate or curative.

6. When administered by skilled clinicians, the safety of long term antibiotic therapy has been firmly established.

The very existence of hundreds of Lyme support groups in this country, and the tens of thousands of dissatisfied, mistreated and ill patients whom these groups represent, underscores the many problems that exist out in the real world of Lyme disease. I ask and plead with you to hear their voices, listen to their stories, and work in an honest and unbiased way to help and protect the many Americans whose health is at risk from what now has become a political disease. Thank you.

As pointed out by the Morgellons Research Foundation, many patients with Morgellons disease have positive Western Blots for Borrelia burgdorferi, the causative agent of Lyme disease. It appears that there may be a connection between the two infectious diseases, with one agent possibly predisposing the individual to the second agent. Whether all patients with Morgellons disease also have Lyme borreliosis remains to be seen. There is some recent information that the fibrous, and other, material associated with skin lesions may be caused by an unknown viral agent or agents.

Ginger Savely, a family nurse practitioner working in a family practice clinic in Austin, Texas, has been seeing patients with Morgellons. These patients have come to her from all over the state of Texas, desperate for answers and willing to go anywhere to be treated with dignity and taken seriously. Savely continues to be impressed with the consistency of their stories. All but one of these patients have tested positive for Lyme borreliosis by Western Blot through IGeneX Laboratories in Palo Alto, California. When she treats these patients with antibiotics for their Lyme disease, she is also seeing remission in Morgellons symptoms in most of her patients.

The true prevalence of Lyme disease is much higher than is being reported by health officials. It is difficult to know how many cases are unreported but estimations suggest that the prevalence is actually 10-15 times higher than what is actually being reported.

Why are health official's under-reporting cases of Lyme disease? Again, the answer is because physicians don't recognize and report most cases. These misdiagnosed cases go unreported even though Lyme disease is a mandatory reportable disease (in the state of Iowa).

A futile cycle exists causing numerous cases of Lyme disease to be misdiagnosed and unreported. That is, since most cases of Lyme disease go undiagnosed, health officials under-report Lyme disease; thus, physicians that read their official reports believe that the prevalence of Lyme is rare and place it low on their list of possibilities when faced with clinical cases that could be caused by Borrelia.

The plague of ignorance surrounding Lyme disease makes it very controversial within the medical community. Most MDs are ignorant about the complex nature of Lyme disease and are frequently irritated when confronted about it.

There are only a few MDs in the country that are knowledgeable about Lyme disease; they are often called Lyme literate MDs (LLMDs) by the Lyme aware public and by their Lyme patients. Most LLMDs know about Lyme disease because they have studied it independently. The MD's formal training in medical school and from the established medical community regarding Lyme disease is meager.

LLMDs have been and continue to be harassed by the medical community, by health officials, by their peers and colleagues, by state medical boards, and by insurance companies for diagnosing and treating

Morgelleons: Level 5 Plague of the New World Order

Lyme patients beyond the standards set by the establishment. Unfortunately, some of these LLMDs have discontinued treating Lyme patients due to the harassment.

A few LLMDs have actually had their medical license revoked because they have treated Lyme patients beyond standards set by the medical community. For example, treating patients with antibiotics for longer than the standard 4-6 week period of time can lead to harassment. A good example of this harassment is the case of Lida Mattman PhD, a microbiologist and author of Stealth Pathogens, was forced to close her Michigan lab in January, 2003. Dr. Mattman, who has studied spirochetes for fifty years, was told by the Michigan state attorney's office to stop helping physicians diagnose Lyme disease in patients, or risk jail time and/or a $5,000 a day fine.

Dr. Mattman has a protocol for culturing the blood of patients, even those who are seronegative for Lyme disease, and is able to find the spirochetes thriving in the blood after a few days incubation. She has helped many patients receive proper antibiotic treatment this way.

She says it has gotten increasingly difficult over the years, to find human negative controls in the U.S. to supply blood free of Borrelia. Dr. Mattman has also recently had the state police arrive at her lab with handcuffs, searching for evidence that she was still doing this work. Fortunately, they did not find the evidence that they were looking for.

Lyme disease affects the nervous system directly and indirectly through the production of neurotoxins. Many patients have had fatigue and poor sleep for years before presenting, and because of strange opportunistic skin infections, it is very easy to mistakenly diagnose them with delusions of parasites. Most labs have inadequate testing for Lyme. Further, there is no known adequate testing for the Piroplasmosis variants, and at least 13 are known to exist.

Those who are brave enough to report their symptoms of Morgellons, find startling similarities with the symptoms of Lyme disease. Symptoms can and may include (but not limited to) involuntary muscle twitches, chronic fatigue, inability to handle stress, low hormone levels, fibromyalgia, (pain and aching of nerve and muscles) muscle spasms, muscle and joint swelling, confusion, mental overload, difficulty concentrating, paralysis sensation, nausea.

Of particular concern with Morgellons is the possibility that it is contagious, unlike Lyme disease. There are cases in the country of multiple family members coming down with the same symptoms. In fact, there is a strong likelihood that if one family member has Morgellons, others will soon follow.

The states of California, Texas and Florida appear to have the highest number of reports of this disease, with primary clusters noted in Los Angeles, San Francisco, Houston, Dallas, and Austin, Texas. All fifty states and fifteen nations, including Canada, the UK, Australia and the Netherlands report cases of Morgellons. The total number of registrations to the Morgellons Research Foundation website is presently 1200, which is believed by the foundation to be a fraction of the actual number of cases.

The two main occupational groups reporting symptoms of Morgellons are nurses and teachers. Nurses outnumber teachers 3:1, but both occupational groups represent a significant percentage of patients with this disease. It is unclear what the risk factors for these two occupational groups might be, but the possibility of casual transmission of infectious agents has been entertained.

There is some evidence to suggest that skin lesions and fibers may not be readily apparent on all individuals with this disease, as family members of patients often report similar systemic disease symptoms, without skin symptoms. Whether the disease is transmissible by human contact remains unclear. Although most sufferers are fearful of infecting family members, families where all are affected are ones where simultaneous mutual exposure is suspected.

Patients have also reported symptoms of this disease in their pets. The majority of reports involve dogs, but cats appear to be increasingly affected. There have also been recent reports of horses with skin lesions fitting the description of Morgellons lesions. Several horse owners have observed fibers associated with skin lesions on their animals, by using lighted 30x handheld microscopes.

Dr. William Harvey is the current chairman of the NASA Education Advisory Committee. He has documented more than 565 of these (Borreliosis) cases in Texas and says 94% of (those with Morgellons' skin lesions) have tested positive for the bacteria associated with Lyme disease, or Borreliosis. "I think we are a looking at a major problem that has been unrecognized in humanity right now."

There has even been the suggestion that Morgellons is a weaponized version of Lyme disease. But where could such a disease be developed?

CHAPTER THREE
Was Morgellons Developed in A Lab?

There have been allegations over the years that Lyme disease was a natural disease made worse by genetic manipulation. The focus of these accusations is Plum Island, Just off Orient Point, Long Island, and six miles from the Connecticut coast.

Plum Island is the site of a United States Agriculture Department Animal Disease Research Center. The USDA acquired the island from the War Department at the end of World War II with a charter from Congress to study and eradicate animal diseases such as Foot and Mouth Disease.

In 1954, research was influenced by the Cold War and scientists began studying ways to inflict damage on Soviet livestock. The Cuban government alleges that in the 1960s and 70s, bioweapons developed at Plum were deployed against Cuban agriculture, targeting pork, tobacco and sugar cane.

Today, Plum Island is home to a Bio-Safety Level 4 (possibly a secret Bio-Safety 5) research facility. The only comparable government facilities in the country are the United States Army laboratory at Fort Detrick, MD, and the Centers for Disease Control and Prevention in Atlanta. Plum Island is specifically engaged in the study of zoonotic diseases. Zoonotic diseases are diseases that can be transmitted from animals to humans, like West Nile, Lyme disease and Ebola.

In surrounding communities, distrust of Plum Island runs deep. Lyme disease takes its name from a Connecticut town across from the island; many wonder whether birds or swimming animals could have brought the disease from Plum Island. Some suspect that it may have been deliberately released. Plum Island officials, of course, dismiss such hypotheses as fantasy.

Citizen concerns do, however, have validation. Even though it is located on an island, Plum Island's lab is not quarantined. Scientists and other laboratory workers commute to Connecticut and Long Island. In August 1994, a worker at Yale's Arbovirus Laboratory became infected with

Sabia Virus but went home and then to Boston before realizing his symptoms was serious.

The risk of accidental exposure would be greater on Plum Island, where instead of cultures in flasks (as at Yale), there are animal populations infected with zoonotic diseases. Such diseases have incubation times of days; a worker could easily go home or travel without realizing that they had been infected.

The government claims that there has only been one outbreak on the island, Foot and Mouth in 1978, which they contained by killing all the livestock. They further maintain that there has never been a leak to the mainland. Apparently the first appearance of Lyme disease, 13-miles northeast of the facility, falls under the category of coincidence, as does the mysterious and still unexplained appearance of West Nile virus in Long Island and New York City.

Until 1991, all of the employees at Plum Island were federal. During 1991 and '92, the workforce divided, with many of the jobs being turned over to the private sector, which naturally led to a simmering resentment in the ranks.

On August 13, 2002, the resentment came to a full boil and a strike was called; 76 members of the International Union of Operating Engineers walked out at midnight after negotiations on wages and benefits broke down. The union members, employed by a government subcontractor, LB&B Associates, headquartered in Columbia, MD, were responsible for essential support services such as decontamination, waste-water treatment, keeping the generators in working order and other maintenance and safety-oriented occupations. For the duration of the strike, temps were brought in to replace them, the sentinels and technicians of the island's infrastructure.

By the end of that month, the FBI had been called to the island to investigate allegations of sabotage. It seems that the water pressure on the island fell precipitously, disabling decontamination facilities and the necropsy rooms used to examine dead animals.

The union blamed the problem on the inexperienced temporary replacement workers, suggesting that they had not been adequately screened and lacked the training to properly maintain the essential daily activity of the island, let alone handle an emergency. Jacob Bunch, a spokesman for LB&B, refused to comment on the FBI investigation and responded to a *New York Times* reporter's query about the replacement workers by stating that "In terms of training, I will tell you that people are well trained or they wouldn't be there. I am not going to get into how they are trained." He flatly refused to discuss the issue of security clearances.

Press requests to visit the island were denied by both the FBI and the USDA, but one union official claimed to have received a frantic call from one of the replacement workers. As he put it, "They were sleeping on cots, working 12-hour shifts and not being able to make calls off the island. He described their condition as being held captive." The chief operating officer of LB&B, Ed Brandon, scoffed at the report, saying that the worker in question had already left the island and that everything was under control and running smoothly.

As a result of the FBI investigation, one of the strikers, Mark J. DePonte, pleaded guilty to tampering with government property. Coincidentally, in October a 600-gallon container of liquid nitrogen somehow managed to tumble off the rear of one of the island's ferries. Shortly thereafter, it was revealed that at least one of the replacement workers had an arrest record.

SECRET WORK WITH MYCOPLASMA

There are 200 species of Mycoplasma. Most do no harm; only four or five are pathogenic. Mycoplasma fermentans (incognitus strain) probably comes from the nucleus of the Brucella bacterium. This disease agent is not a bacterium and not a virus; it is a mutated form of the Brucella bacterium, combined with a visna virus, from which the mycoplasma is extracted.

The pathogenic Mycoplasma used to be innocuous, but biological warfare research conducted between 1942 and the present time has resulted in the creation of more deadly and infectious forms of Mycoplasma. Researchers extracted this mycoplasma from the Brucella bacterium and actually reduced the disease to a crystalline form. It was then probably weaponised and tested it on an unsuspecting public in the United States.

Dr. LeeAnn Thomas, the previous Director of Plum Island, told author Marjorie Tietjen that Iraqi researcher, Dr. Jawad Al Aubaidi, (who has since been murdered) did his graduate training at Plum Island, specifically involving different strains of mycoplasma. He went back to Iraq and headed up the mycoplasma research program at the University of Bagdad.

Tiejen had been sent information from a reliable source that stated that 60% of chronic lyme patients are co-infected with several strains of mycoplasma, the most common one being "mycoplasma fermentens" which is patented by the U.S. Army and army pathologist Dr. Shyh-Ching Lo (Pathogenic mycoplasma-U.S. Patent 5,242,820 issued Sept. 7, 1993).

Tiejen writes in her article: ***Living Next Door To Plum Island*** that it is evident that any microbe that has been "modified" is considered "off limits" for treatment and any physician that takes these chronic infections seriously, is targeted for harassment. This same pathogen is found in Gulf War Illness, Fibromyalgia, Chronic Fatigue patients, and maybe Morgellons.

Tietjen asked Dr. Thomas if Plum Island ever worked with mycoplasmas in general. She denied this at the beginning but gradually admitted researching seven different strains. Tuethen asked if Plum Island researchers ever worked with mycoplasma fermentens. Dr. Thomas was immediately familiar with that particular genetically engineered strain although she did deny that Plum Island researchers ever worked with it.

According to accurate and verified accounts, Saddam Hussein purchased mycoplasma as well as other biologicals, which included West Nile Virus, from the U.S. right up to two weeks before Desert Storm.

West Nile virus infection in humans first broke out in New York City in August, 1999. The first sign of the disease occurred in early July when half the crows in the New York City area died, as well as some exotic bird species housed at the Bronx zoo.

A few weeks after the bird deaths, the first human cases of encephalitis appeared in local hospitals in the northern Queens section of the city. By September, nine of 25 infected horses with WN virus died in Long Island.

It was later discovered that mosquito's acts as a carrier for the virus, thus it spreads from birds to mosquitoes. The virus then is spread to humans and other animals by mosquito bites.

Although the virus is contagious between birds, the disease is not contagious between humans. It is estimated that only 20% of infected people will develop a mild flu-like form of the illness; but one in 150 people will develop a severe form of the disease with mental confusion, headache, swollen glands, high fever, severe muscle weakness, and the tell-tale symptoms of encephalitis (inflammation of the brain). Mild cases last a few days; severe cases can last several weeks.

In 1999, the disease was completely confined to the New York City area, with 62 cases and 7 deaths. As many as 10,000 wild birds died. In the year 2000, there were 21 cases and two deaths; in 2001 there were 56 cases with 7 deaths. By October 8, 2002 the CDC had reported a cumulative total of 2768 cases of WN virus with 146 deaths; and it is estimated that as many as 200,000 people are infected nationally.

Until 2002 the virus was confined to states in the eastern half of the country. By the summer of 2002, all but 6 of the lower 48 states reported West Nile virus in birds, mosquitoes, animals or humans. It has caused nearly 17,000 cases of illness in people, more than 650 of them fatal.

Secret CIA documents point the finger at Iraq as being responsible for the West Nile virus outbreak in the United States. Health officials believe the West Nile virus may have been genetically altered into an illness far deadlier to human beings. Interestingly, the U.S. strain appears almost identical to only one other strain in the world – the one found in Israel.

In most parts of the world where it has surfaced, the virus typically causes illness akin to the flu, bringing fever, headache, muscle aches and fatigue – unpleasant, but rarely fatal. The virus has not even proven fatal to all birds in other parts of the world. But the U.S. strain appears nearly 100 percent fatal to birds. They usually die within five days.

Once again, this has caused some health officials and scientists, as well as intelligence sources, to wonder if West Nile Virus is not a weaponized virus – one perhaps deliberately engineered and delivered to the two biggest targets of Islamic terrorism. Israel was the first place in the world where West Nile virus was associated with killing birds. Until that outbreak in 1997, the virus was known to sicken birds, but not fatally. Israel also was the site of an outbreak of West Nile virus in humans that caused 450 cases of neurological disease in 2000.

While it is well-known that West Nile virus is of Middle East origin, what is less well-known is the New Yorker report dating back to 2000 in which Saddam Hussein was quoted by a defector referring to "his final weapon, developed in laboratories outside Iraq...free of U.N. inspection, the laboratories will develop strain SV 141 of the West Nile virus." There is also a report that the Centers for Disease Control actually sent West Nile virus samples to Iraq in 1985.

One entomology expert who maintains an open mind on the West Nile outbreak, Dr. Jonathan F. Day of the University of Florida, said: "The sporadic appearance of West Nile virus is disturbing. It really appears that the virus has been seeded throughout the eastern half of the United States. I guess the question is, by whom?"

It is not too far outside of the spectrum to suggest that Morgellons could be a manmade disease related to Lyme and West Nile. One woman, identified by the name "L," sent the author an e-mail stating that her husband, in 1993/1994, worked as a mechanical technician for a chemical plant that started an experimental program for their wastewater treatment plant adding plant organisms into their wastewater treatment facility.

"He assisted with the installation of the startup equipment and overlooked the ongoing maintenance of this equipment. There were times he would be working on this equipment in nothing more than rubber boots and a dust mask. This plant organism was not supposed to infect humans."

"L" and her husband have both come down with symptoms of Morgellons. From the research so far, scientists who are examining the lesions and the fibers extracted from them are finding that the fibers might be made of cellulose, a molecule generally found in plants.

Another source reported that Morgellons had been researched by the Chinese since 1994. Their findings were nematodes that had been genetically modified in the use at waste water treatment plants were the cause of the disease.

Nematodes are a good candidate for Mogellons, whether natural or genetically modified. They can be hard to spot, are sometimes infectious, have several species known to infest humans, and have produced other baffling cases.

One of the strangest cases is the multi-limbed frogs in Minnesota. Turns out, they were infested with nematodes while they were tadpoles; every spot where a nematode had lived for some reason developed into a leg when the frog metamorphosed into an adult. The reason they had suddenly become a problem was because of dramatic changes in the local ecosystem, mainly brought about by man, which led to a nematode population explosion.

CUSTOM-BUILT PATHOGENS RAISE BIOTERROR FEARS

The Washington Post reported on July 31, 2006 that terrorists could someday use a shortcut to get their hands on the lethal viruses that cause Ebola and smallpox. Eckard Wimmer knows this because he discovered it himself. In 2002, the German-born molecular geneticist startled the scientific world by creating the first live, fully artificial virus in the lab. It was a variation of the bug that causes polio, yet different from any virus known to nature. And Wimmer built it from scratch.

The virus was made from nonliving parts, using equipment and chemicals on hand in Wimmer's small laboratory at the State University of New York on Long Island. The most crucial part, the genetic code, was picked up for free on the Internet. Hundreds of tiny bits of viral DNA were purchased online, with final assembly in the lab.

Wimmer intended to sound a warning, to show that science had crossed a threshold into an era in which genetically altered and made-from-scratch germ weapons were feasible. But in the four years since, other scientists have made advances faster than Wimmer imagined possible. Government officials, and scientists such as Wimmer, are only beginning to grasp the implications.

The new technology opens the door to new tools for defeating disease and saving lives. But today, in hundreds of labs worldwide, it is also possible to transform common intestinal microbes into killers. Or to make deadly strains even more lethal…or to resurrect bygone killers, such the 1918 influenza…or to manipulate a person's hormones by switching genes on or off…or to craft cheap, efficient delivery systems that can infect large numbers of people.

The U.S. Centers for Disease Control and Prevention has declined so far to police the booming gene-synthesis industry, which churns out made-to-order DNA to sell to scientists. Oversight of controversial experiments remains voluntary and sporadic in many universities and private labs in the United States, and occurs even more rarely overseas.

Wimmer's artificial virus looks and behaves like its natural cousin – but with a far reduced ability to maim or kill – and could be used to make a safer polio vaccine. However, it was Wimmer's techniques, not his aims that sparked controversy when news of his achievement reached the scientific journals.

As the creator of the world's first "de novo" virus – a human virus, at that–Wimmer came under attack from other scientists who said his experiment was a dangerous stunt. He was accused of giving ideas to terrorists, or, even worse, of inviting a backlash that could result in new laws restricting scientific freedom.

Wimmer counters that he didn't invent the technology that made his experiment possible. He only drew attention to it.

New techniques developed by other scientists allow the creation of synthetic viruses in mere days, not weeks or months. Hardware unveiled last year by a Harvard genetics professor can churn out synthetic genes by the thousands, for a few pennies each.

In less than five years, synthetic biology has gone from a kind of scientific parlor trick, useful for such things as creating glow-in-the-dark fish, to a cutting-edge bioscience with enormous commercial potential. Now the technology can be even done at the lab bench in high school.

Along with synthetic biologists, a separate but equally ardent group is pursuing DNA shuffling, a kind of directed evolution that imbues microbes with new traits. Still another group is discovering ways to manipulate the essential biological circuitry of humans, using chemicals or engineered microbes to shut down defective genes or regulate the production of hormones controlling such functions as metabolism and mood.

Could a biowarfare weapons lab, such as Plum Island, have managed to create a new, weaponized version of Lymes disease that we are now calling Morgellons? Did they manage to genetically combine Lymes with a plant organism used in wastewater treatment to create a brand new disease? Is the population of the U.S. unwittingly acting as guinea pigs to this manmade sickness?

The symptoms of Morgellons, especially the fibers and feelings of bugs crawling and biting under the skin, are certainly odd and not what would be considered an effective biowarfare weapon. In biowarfare, the idea is to incapacitate, or even kill, the enemy so that they cannot resist an invading army. So far, Morgellons does not seem to be a fatal disease. However, as it progresses, its victims are left weak, helpless and possibly even contagious.

Maybe Morgellons is a new example of 21st century biowarfare, where instead of death; a population is rendered helpless with disease.

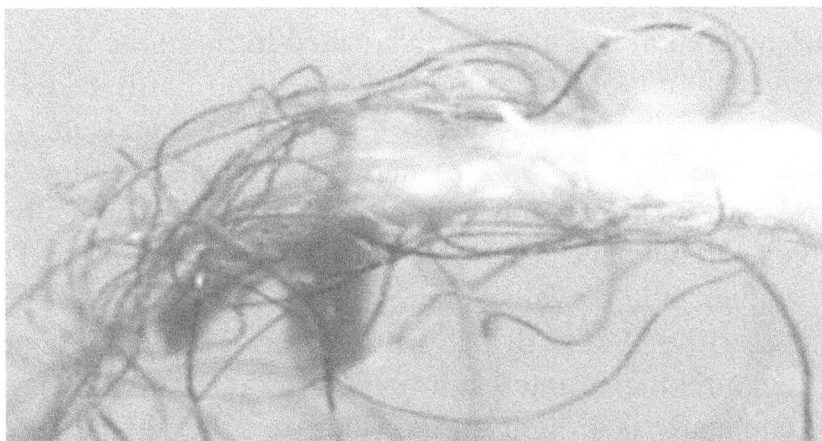

The strange threads of Morgellons
could show a man-made connection.

CHAPTER FOUR
Is Morgellons From Outer Space?

Did life on Earth originate from outer space? Do new diseases such as Morgellons rain down on us on a daily basis, with some taking hold with a frightening vengeance?

The term Panspermian, meaning literally, "seeds everywhere" was first suggested by the Greek philosopher Anaxagoras, who influenced Socrates. However, Aristotle's theory of spontaneous generation came to be preferred by science for more than two thousand years.

On April 9, 1864, French chemist Louis Pasteur announced his great experiment disproving spontaneous generation as it was then held to occur. In the 1870s, British physicist Lord Kelvin and German physicist Hermann von Helmholtz reinforced Pasteur and argued that life could come from space. And in the first decade of the 1900s, Swedish chemist and Nobel laureate Svante Arrhenius theorized that bacterial spores propelled through space by light pressure were the seeds of life on Earth.

In the 1920s, Russian biochemist Alexander Oparin and English geneticist J.B.S. Haldane, writing independently, revived the doctrine of spontaneous generation in a more sophisticated form. In the new version, the spontaneous generation of life no longer happens on Earth, takes too long to observe in a laboratory, and has left no clues about its occurrence. Supporting this theory, in 1953, American chemists Stanley Miller and Harold Urey showed that some amino acids can be chemically produced from ammonia and methane. That experiment is now famous, and the Oparin - Haldane paradigm still prevails today.

Starting in the 1970s, British astronomers Fred Hoyle and Chandra Wickramasinghe rekindled interest in panspermia. By careful spectroscopic observation and analysis of light from distant stars they found new evidence, traces of life, in the intervening dust. They also proposed that comets, which are largely made of water-ice, carry bacterial life across galaxies and protect it from radiation damage along the way. One aspect of this research program, that interstellar dust and comets contain organic compounds, has been pursued by others as well. It is now universally accepted that space contains the "ingredients" of life. This development could be the first hint of a huge paradigm shift. But mainstream science has not accepted the hard core of modern panspermia, that whole cells seeded life on Earth.

Hoyle and Wickramasinghe also broadened or generalized panspermia to include a new understanding of evolution. While accepting the fact that life on Earth evolved over the course of about four billion years, they say that the genetic programs for higher evolution cannot be explained by random mutation and recombination among genes for single-celled organisms, even in that long a time: the programs must come from somewhere beyond Earth.

In a nutshell, their theory holds that all of life comes from space. It incorporates the original panspermia in the same way that General Relativity incorporates Special Relativity. Their expanded theory can well be termed "strong" panspermia.

LIFE ON EARTH

Most scientists have long assumed that life developed and evolved on Earth. According to the conventional hypothesis, the earliest living cells emerged as a result of chemical evolution on our planet billions of years ago in a process called abiogenesis.

The alternative possibility that living cells or their precursors arrived from space strikes many people as science fiction. Developments over the past decade, however, have given new credibility to the idea that Earth's biosphere could have arisen from an extra-terrestrial seed.

Planetary scientists have learned that early in its history, our solar system could have included many worlds with liquid water, the essential ingredient for life as we know it. Recent data from NASA's Mars Exploration Rovers corroborate previous suspicions that water has at least intermittently flowed on the Red Planet in the past.

It is not unreasonable to hypothesize that life existed on Mars long ago and perhaps continues there. Life may have also evolved on Europa, Jupiter's fourth-largest moon, which appears to possess liquid water under its icy surface. Saturn's biggest satellite, Titan, is rich in organic compounds; given the moon's frigid temperatures, it would be highly surprising to find living forms there, but they cannot be ruled out.

Life may have even gained a toehold on torrid Venus. The Venusian surface is probably too hot and under too much atmospheric pressure to be habitable, but the planet could conceivably support microbial life high in its atmosphere. And most likely, the surface conditions on Venus were not always so harsh.

Venus may have once been similar to early Earth. Moreover, the expanses of interplanetary space are not the forbidding barrier they once seemed. Over the past 20 years, scientists have determined that more than 30 meteorites found on Earth originally came from the Martian crust, based on the composition of gases trapped within some of the rocks.

Meanwhile, biologists have discovered organisms durable enough to survive at least a short journey inside such meteorites. Although no one is suggesting that these particular organisms actually made the trip, they serve as a proof of principle.

It is not implausible that life could have arisen on Mars and then come to Earth, or the reverse. Researchers are now intently studying the transport of biological materials between planets to get a better sense of whether it ever occurred. This effort may shed light on some of modern science's most compelling questions: Where and how did life originate? Are radically different forms of life possible? And how common is life in the universe?

In its modern form, the panspermia hypothesis addresses how biological material might have arrived on our planet, but not how life originated in the first place. No matter where it started, life had to arise from non-living matter.

A biogenesis moved from the realm of philosophy to that of experimentation in the 1950s, when chemists Stanley L. Miller and Harold C. Urey of the University of Chicago demonstrated that amino acids and other molecules important to life could be generated from simple compounds believed to exist on early Earth. It is now thought that molecules of ribonucleic acid (RNA) could have also assembled from smaller compounds and played a vital role in the development of life. In present-day cells, specialized RNA molecules help to build proteins. Some RNAs act as messengers between the genes, which are made of deoxyribonucleic acid (DNA), and the ribosomes, the protein factories of the cell.

In the early stages of life's evolution, all the enzymes may have been RNAs, not proteins. Because RNA enzymes could have manufactured the first proteins without the need for preexisting protein enzymes to initiate the process, abiogenesis is not the chicken-and-egg problem that it was once thought to be.

Morgelleons: Level 5 Plague of the New World Order

A prebiotic system of RNAs and proteins could have gradually developed the ability to replicate its molecular parts, crudely at first, but then ever more efficiently. This new understanding of life's origins has transformed the scientific debate over panspermia. It is no longer an either or question of whether the first microbes arose on Earth or arrived from space.

In the chaotic early history of the solar system, our planet was subject to intense bombardment by meteorites containing simple organic compounds. The young Earth could have also received more complex molecules with enzymatic functions, molecules that were prebiotic but part of a system that was already well on its way to biology.

After landing in a suitable habitat on our planet, these molecules could have continued their evolution to living cells. In other words, an intermediate scenario is possible: life could have roots both on Earth and in space. But which steps in the development of life occurred where? And once life took hold, how far did it spread?

Scientists who study panspermia used to concentrate only on assessing the basic plausibility of the idea, but they have recently sought to estimate the probability that biological materials made the journey to Earth from other planets or moons. To begin their interplanetary trip, the materials would have to be ejected from their planet of origin into space by the impact of a comet or asteroid.

While traveling through space, the ejected rocks or dust particles would need to be captured by the gravity of another planet or moon, then decelerated enough to fall to the surface, passing through the atmosphere if one were present. Such transfers happen frequently throughout the solar system, although it is easier for ejected material to travel from bodies more distant from the sun to those closer in and easier for materials to end up on a more massive body. Indeed, dynamic simulations by University of British Columbia astrophysicist Brett Gladman suggest that the mass transferred from Earth to Mars is only a few percent of that delivered from Mars to Earth. For this reason, the most commonly discussed panspermia scenario involves the transport of microbes or their precursors from Mars to Earth.

IS MORGELLONS FROM MARS?

The symptoms of Morgellons certainly seem almost out of this world, creepy-crawly feelings under the skin, strange lesions that do not heal, and unusual thread-like material that exudes from the skin wounds. People from all over the globe are reporting the very same symptoms, and doctors are baffled.

What makes Morgellons so unique are the weird fibers that grow out of the victim's skin. No other disease known on Earth has this bizarre symptom. So could this mean that Morgellons could have originated somewhere other than Earth?

Mike Moore, who runs the website: marslife.com, believes that this is the case and that Morgellons could have traveled to Earth on a meteorite.

But not just any meteorites, meteorites from Mars.

In the winter of 1970/71 Moore found a meteorite on a ranch in Texas. After careful study, Moore concluded that the unusual rock had formed under extremely dry conditions and was volcanic in origin. He believes that it came to Earth by the result of the impact of a large asteroid onto the surface of Mars.

"When I first found the meteorite, it had just come through our atmosphere, and the outer surface had probably been 'sterilized' by the high heat that melted the entire outer surface of the meteorite," Moore says. "It wasn't until 10 or 15 years later that I noticed that some 'fuzz' or 'filaments' were coming out of the crevice that runs through one side of the meteorite."

Moore was confused about what he was seeing. How could a rock from Mars be growing something that appeared to be alive? It was not until NASA announced in 1996 that they had found the possible remnants of life in a Martian meteorite that he began to consider that what he was seeing was some kind of Martian life growing on his meteorite. When he broke off a small sample of the meteorite, "sand" fell out.

Using a pocket microscope he found a piece of something that had obviously come from some kind of plant, or at least a living thing. It very obviously represented the remains of life of some kind and it had come from the meteorite. Attached to it was a filament. When he looked at it under the microscope and then looked at the fuzz coming out of the crevice, it seemed to Moore that they were the same "creature."

Moore spent several months at the Roswell UFO museum in New Mexico, where a worker offered to do some tests on the meteorite's contents. Moore gave him a small sample of sand that had fallen from the middle of the meteorite.

When the pile was examined under a microscope, it was apparent that the filament creatures were present in the sample. While trying to glue one end of one of the filament creature to a slide for study under the microscope, the filament moved back and forth, as if trying to avoid being stuck to the slide. Morgellons patients have also reported a similar movement of the "threads" and "fibers" that are associated with their disease.

Moore speculates that rocks blown off of Mars have been falling to Earth throughout history, bringing with them the minute life forms that we now call Morgellons. What still needs to be answered is whether or not Morgellons adapted itself to Earth conditions millions of years ago, or if it is a relatively "new" condition that has surfaced over the last few centuries.

There is also the feeling, according to Moore, that the Morgellons filaments almost seem intelligent. First, if one looks at their "constructions" one would have to think their behavior was deliberate.

"I often find them 'winding' along the walls of the vesicles of the rock. They have grown or moved to fit the walls of the vesicles and in the inner vesicles of the rock actually make 3D structures within the vesicles, extending from wall to wall and supporting structures in the middle."

It seems to Moore that they are collecting silicon: "It appears that tiny little panes of glass are being formed on the outside of the creatures."

Moore feels that the Morgellons creatures are not harmful and are in fact serving a good purpose by going after tiny insects that are already infesting their human host. However, nothing conclusive can be discovered until scientists accept the idea that Morgellons is real and does the proper research needed to find out once and for all if there is a connection between Morgellons and meteorites from the planet Mars.

RED RAIN OVER INDIA

Modern reports of Morgellons first surfaced in 2002. Strangely, Kerala, India may have had an extraterrestrial encounter in a mysterious red rain that fell in 2001.

Professor Godfrey Louis, at the School of Pure and Applied Physics of the Mahatma Gandhi University, said that: "Analyzing the red rain sample under an optical microscope, I found that it had cell appearances. Then I placed it under a transmission electron microscope and found that it had a detailed cell structure and a fine wall membrane."

Professor Louis, who published his findings in the *Astrophysics and Space Science*, Netherlands journal in November 2005, also noted that when he looked through a scanning electron microscope the sample showed the external morphology and it had a biological structure.

The professor found strange, thick-walled, red-tinted cell-like structures about 10 microns in size. Stranger still, dozens of his experiments suggest that the particles may lack DNA yet still reproduce plentifully, even in water superheated to nearly 600?F. (The known upper limit for life in water is about 250 degrees F.)

Louis speculates that the particles could be extraterrestrial bacteria adapted to the harsh conditions of space and that the microbes hitched a ride on a comet or meteorite that later broke apart in the upper atmosphere and mixed with rain clouds above India. If his theory proves correct, the cells would be the first confirmed evidence of alien life and, as such, could yield tantalizing new clues to the origins of life on Earth.

The story of the strange red rain began on July 25, 2001, when residents of Kerala, a state in southwestern India, started seeing scarlet rain in some areas.

"Almost the entire state, except for two northern districts, have reported these unusual rains over the past week," the BBC online reported on July 30. "Experts said the most likely reason was the presence of dust in the atmosphere which colors the water."

However, the explanation didn't satisfy everyone. The rain "is eluding explanations as the days go by," the newspaper *Indian Express* reported online a week later.

The article said the Centre for Earth Science Studies, based in Thiruvananthapuram, India, had discarded an initial hypothesis that a streaking meteor triggered the rain, in favor of the view that the particles were spores from a fungus. But "the exact species is yet to be identified. [And] how such a large quantity of spores could appear over a small region is as yet unknown," the paper quoted center director M. Baba as saying.

The red rain continued to appear sporadically for about two months, though most of it fell in the first 10 days. The striking red coloration turned out to come from microscopic, mixed-in red particles that had no similarity with usual desert dust.

It has been estimated that at least 55 tons of the particles have fallen in all. An analysis of this strange phenomenon further shows that the conventional atmospheric transport processes like dust storms etc. cannot explain it. Professor Louis speculates that a meteor may be responsible for the red particles.

The red rain phenomenon first started in Kerala after a meteor airburst event, which occurred on July 25, 2001 near Changanacherry in the Kottayam district. This meteor airburst is evidenced by a sonic boom heard by a number people during the early morning of that day.

Morgelleons: Level 5 Plague of the New World Order

"The first case of red rain occurred in this area few hours after the airburst. This points to a possible link between the meteor and red rain. If particle clouds are created in the atmosphere by the fragmentation and disintegration of a special kind of fragile cometary meteor that presumably contains a dense collection of red particles, then clouds of such particles can mix with the rain clouds to cause red rain," Professor Louis wrote.

It has been suggested that while approaching Earth at low angle, the meteor traveled southeast above Kerala with a final airburst above the Kottayam district. During its travel in the atmosphere it must have released several small fragments, which caused the deposition of cell clusters in the atmosphere.

Strangely, a test for DNA using Ethidium Bromide dye fluorescence technique indicates an absence of DNA in these cells. Nonetheless, Professor Louis wrote that the particles show "fine-structured membranes" under magnification, like normal cells.

"The major constituents of the red particles are carbon and oxygen," he wrote. "Silicon is most prominent among the minor constituents of the particles."

Chandra Wickramasinghe, director of the Cardiff Centre for Astrobiology at Cardiff University, U.K., thinks that a more careful examination of the red rain material is needed, but feels that at first glance, there is good evidence that the red rain could have extraterrestrial origins.

This is not the first time that Wickramasinghe has suggested that certain diseases may have their origins in outer space. Wickramasinghe and his colleagues suggest in a letter to the scientific journal *The Lancet* that the SARS virus may have arrived with 2,200 pounds of bacterial material that fall to the planet every day. That's 20,000 bacteria per square meter of the Earth's surface.

Some of this material is "highly evolved, with an evolutionary history closely related to life that exists on Earth," Wickramasinghe wrote in the letter. This, he wrote, "raises the possibility that pathogenic bacteria and viruses might also be introduced."

Epidemiologists, virologists, genomic researchers and other scientists worldwide have been working around the clock to track the origin of SARS and stem its spread. But if Wickramasinghe is correct in his space theory, their efforts may be moot.

"New cases might continue to appear until the stratospheric supply of the causative agent becomes exhausted," he wrote.

Morgelleons: Level 5 Plague of the New World Order

Medical history is rife with plagues and pestilences that could be attributed to space microbes, he said. He cited epidemics such as the plague of Athens, the plague of Justinian and the flu epidemic of 1918 as other outbreaks that could be space-induced, because they appeared and retreated abruptly.

"The patterns of spread of these diseases, as charted by historians, are often difficult to explain simply on the basis of endemic infective agents," he wrote.

He and his colleagues collected bacteria from a balloon launched from the Indian Space Research Organization and Tata Institute Balloon Facility in Hyderabad, India, on Jan. 21, 2001. This data showing how much bacteria entered the atmosphere from space led them to theorize that extraterrestrial disease-causing agents could affect the biosphere.

"A small amount of the culprit virus introduced into the stratosphere," he wrote, "could make a first tentative fall out east of the great mountain range of the Himalayas where the stratosphere is thinnest, followed by sporadic deposits in neighboring areas."

Matthew Genge, of the Department of Mineralogy at the London Natural History Museum, has estimated the amount of comet dust that survives entry into the lower atmosphere, and thus how frequently an average-sized human might be struck.

Genge figures that if you live to be 5,000 years old, you'll likely encounter one comet dust particle. Were it to harbor a virus, you would presumably have to inhale the particle, further reducing the odds of infection.

"Comet dust particles constantly rain from the skies -- around a hundred thousand billion particles per year -- and some of these will fall on people," Genge told space.com, adding that the extremely light particles would probably not be noticed. Genge said that some of the dust particles could contain bio-molecules.

It is no stretch of the imagination then to suggest that Morgellons, as well as other unexplained and mysterious diseases may have arrived on Earth from the darkest regions of outer space. Considering how life is able to gain a foothold in some of the most inhospitable regions on the Earth, it is possible that the harsh realm of space is no barrier for life as it seeks to establish itself all across the universe.

CHAPTER FIVE
All in Their Heads

Even though sufferers of Morgellons display symptoms that are plainly apparent for all to see, most doctors refuse to believe that their patients are really suffering from a physiological illness. Instead, victims are often ignored or worst yet, told that their problems are psychological and not physical. If there is no insurance code into which the medical practitioner can "slot" a condition…it does not exist except as a delusional disorder.

Delusional parasitosis was first described in scientific detail and terms by Karl Ekbom, a Swedish neurologist, in 1937 and 1938. The form of delusional parasitosis described by Ekbom involves the conviction that parasites inhabit the skin, and this remains the most commonly encountered manifestation of the illness.

Those suffering from delusions of parasitosis believe that they are infected by parasites, insects and bugs. They report feelings of crawling bugs, stinging, biting or burrowing into the skin, and often causing itchy rashes and/or painful lesions that last for weeks or months and leave permanent scars.

Physicians distinguish between primary delusions of parasitosis, which occurs without any other underlying physical or mental disorder, and secondary delusions of parasitosis, which occurs as a result or symptom (or set of symptoms) of another condition, such as diabetes or schizophrenia. As unlikely as this condition seems, to doctors and entomologists, it is a reality. Ekbom said it was true. Since his article, physicians have essentially echoed him, without adding any scientific evidence to the theory.

Although some writers say that patients suffering from true delusional parasitosis exhibit no lesions on the skin, most acknowledge that they have seen the sores, rashes, and other evidence of an actual skin disease. Obvious bumps, rashes, etc., are sometimes explained as the result of "stress," acne, dry skin, contact dermatitis, or ordinary insect bites. However, sufferers are often described as having caused these skin problems themselves by excoriating or attempts at extermination or, as one source call it, self mutilation.

Some descriptions of this behavior are quite specific: "Excoriations are classically produced by the fingernails and there may also be signs of chemical burns as a result of attempts to kill the parasites. The patient is compelled to dig the parasites out, especially before going to bed, and often resorts to the use of a knife, tweezers or other sharp implement, leaving skin lesions consistent therewith."

Those that suffer from Morgellons have been told by their doctors that they had caused their own lesions even in places on their backs that they could not reach. Denying this behavior is pointless. "Self-excoriation is a common feature of delusory parasitosis, despite the individuals' protests that they do not scratch, doctors are quick to dismiss their patients complaints.

A circular logic is at work here. Attempting to remove parasites can only be evidence of being delusional if one already knows the parasites themselves are delusionary. A non-delusional individual truly infected by a skin parasite would behave in exactly the same way. It is only because the doctors have already decided that sufferers of Morgellons are delusional and that their behavior can be used to prove that they are delusional.

The single possible exception is scabies, and scabies does not really produce the same symptoms as Morgellons, and can be completely eradicated with one or two treatments with permethrin cream, a neurotoxin. If anything survives the treatment, it can't be scabies, the reasoning goes, and therefore must be a delusion.

MATCHBOX SIGN

Morgellons victim Jane Waldoch, a nurse for 24 year says she finds fibers that look like crunched up bugs in her sheets every morning. They come from the dozens of sores that cover her arms, legs, back and neck.

She began collecting samples of what was coming out of her skin. She thought it would help her doctors diagnose this bizarre and painful skin condition. She was wrong. Instead, Doctors took it as a sign that Jane was delusional.

"One of the hallmark clues to delusional parasitosis is what they call the matchbox sign. I guess in the older days people would take their samples in little match boxes to their physician," she says.

Mary Leitao, a biologist and the executive director of the Morgellons Research Foundation, said doctors have become "a brick wall. They have their answer, and they aren't open to discussing the possibility they could be wrong."

"They are so smug and sure they are right," she said.

Dr. Peter Lynch of the University of California, a dermatologist for 40 years, is one of the few skeptical experts who have been willing to even talk on the record. Others have ignored e-mails and telephone calls. He said "If there were a peer-reviewed study, with 15 or 20 patients who have the same exact thing in their skins, then maybe I'd believe it,"

"When fiberglass curtains first came out, many people with skin conditions were diagnosed with delusions of parasitosis (DOP), but studies showed these patients had tiny (fiberglass particles) in their skin."

Although it may seem perfectly reasonable for a person to bring a specimen for a doctor to examine, to do so with a skin disease turns out to be the most damning evidence of the patient's delusional condition. Called the "matchbox sign," or more recently by up-to-date dermatologists, the "Saran-wrap syndrome" or the "Ziploc sign," bringing in skin particles or materials found on or in the skin will carve the diagnosis of delusions into stone. Once again, perfectly normal behavior, based, in fact, on the "scientific method," becomes labeled as pathological.

INSECTS UNDER THE SKIN

A study conducted under the auspices of the National Pediculosis Association (NPA) in Needham, Mass., and the Oklahoma State Department of Health has found that ninety percent of patients with Morgellons were found to have Collembola, also known as Springtails, an almost microscopic insect with six legs, antennas, and no wings. Collembola feed on algae, fungi, bacteria and decaying matter.

The findings were reported in the edition of the *Journal of the New York Entomological Association*. The new findings bolster the contention of many patients that they "actually have something crawling on or under their skin and are not delusional," said the journal article.

Collembola predominately dwell in soil and litter, preferring wet or damp surroundings. They sometimes congregate in large numbers under leaky kitchen or bathroom sinks, swimming pools or in the soil of potted plants. Little is known about the health effects of Collembola, or how to prevent or treat them as a problem for human skin.

Lobelia Sharp, a plant pathologist at the University of California San Francisco, said she's had the lesions, fibers and other symptoms for about six months. When she sought medical help, she was diagnosed with delusional parasitosis, given antidepressants and taken by ambulance to the hospital and held in the mental ward.

She said she and a friend who is a mold scientist recently spent an evening using tweezers to snag "filaments" out of her skin welts and examine them under a microscope. The material – which she said was cellulose plant fibers – was similar to each other but unlike anything either of them had ever seen.

Dr. Noah Scheinfeld, from Columbia University, says Morgellons is not real. He says it's all in the patients head. Dr. Scheinfeld says, "This is somebody who is picking at themselves and people pick at themselves for all sorts of reasons." He says once patients create a sore they shove fibers into it.

Doctors such as Scheinfeld also say it's unlikely that the varied symptoms associated with Morgellons, from lesions to joint pain to loss of vision, could all be caused by the same disease. What's more likely is that as word of Morgellons spreads through the Internet and television news coverage, more people become convinced they have it. If this is the case, then Morgellons is one in a long line of weird diseases that have swept through populations, only to disappear without a trace once public concern subsides.

But Morgellons has not disappeared and a few doctors are now conducting the proper research to try and figure out the mystery once and for all. Beginning in early 2006, 14 Morgellons patients came to the lab of Randy Wymore, assistant professor of pharmacology at Oklahoma State University. Six are children and eight are adults. All have fibers that appear to be growing from their skin.

To prove that the fibers are not environmental contaminants, Wymore and his staff, which includes a doctor and a pediatrician, cut into the skin and remove colored fibers. "To find fibers underneath unbroken skin where there's no lesion, no scarring, no sign of scratching whatsoever, would preclude any possibility of this being contaminants from the environment," Wymore says.

He sends the fibers to an independent pathology lab in Tulsa. During the testing process the fibers are accidentally drained down a sink. He sent another batch in June and is still awaiting the results.

In the last few months, Wymore has been bombarded by phone calls and e-mails from Morgellons sufferers, family members and co-workers, even school principals who wonder if the disease is contagious. Doctors

Morgelleons: Level 5 Plague of the New World Order

from all over the country have called, asking him how they should treat the disease. Since May, he has received 486 e-mails asking for some help or information. He wonders why the CDC isn't doing more.

"Why am I the one dealing with these people?" he asks. "I have no problem dealing with people in Oklahoma as a sort of public service aspect of my job, but when it starts coming from New York and California and Washington and Minnesota, I mean, we've crossed state lines, it seems to me this should become a federal issue."

CIA informants have revealed that Morgellons could be a manmade disease that is being propagated by the secret elite group that controls the world through manipulation of war, money, wealth and poverty...the New World Order. Rumor has it that Morgellons is one of several diseases that have been released in order to create panic in the general population.

It currently appears that Morgellons is not as such a fatal disease, though some sufferers have committed suicide because of the maddening symptoms. However, the psychological impact of Morgellons is real and a serious concern.

Considering the current world situation, terrorist attacks, domestic spying, governments out of control and suppressing democracy and freedoms guaranteed by our founding fathers. It should come to no surprise that the New World Order could stoop to such evil as releasing a disease such as Morgellons upon an unsuspecting planet in order to create panic and chaos. Sometimes the smallest thing can cause the biggest problems. We have to take a deeper look, beyond the affliction itself, before we will find the answers – answers for which we are made to beg.

We cannot allow the truth about Morgellons to be swept under the rug with blanket dismissals of crazy and delusional. We fail in this task at our peril and with the ultimate cost of our health and lives.

For more information about Morgellons, please visit the Morgellons Research Foundation website: http://www.morgellons.org/

Write for our free catalog at:
Global Communications
P.O. Box 753
New Brunswick, NJ 08903
www.conspiracyjournal.com

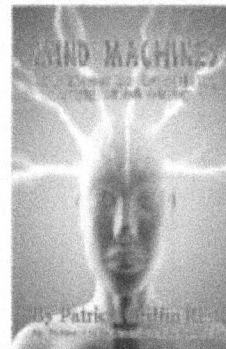

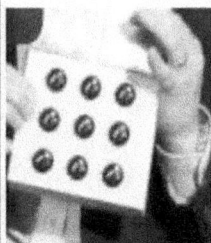